Worry Monsters

Fun activities for kids aged 4+

A child's guide to coping with their feelings

WORRY MONSTERS

Text by Anna Prudente-Poulton and Anna Martin
Design by Julie Goldsmith and Nia Williams
Peer reviewed by Amanda Ashman-Wymbs, BACP Accredited and Registered Counsellor and Psychotherapist

An Hachette UK Company
www.hachette.co.uk

Vie Books, an imprint of Summersdale Publishers Ltd
Part of Octopus Publishing Group Limited
Carmelite House
50 Victoria Embankment
LONDON
EC4Y 0DZ
UK

www.summersdale.com

Printed and bound in China

ISBN: 978-1-80007-559-7

Substantial discounts on bulk quantities of Summersdale books are available to corporations, professional associations and other organizations. For details contact general enquiries: telephone: +44 (0) 1243 771107 or email: enquiries@summersdale.com.

Disclaimer
Neither the author nor the publisher can be held responsible for any loss or claim arising out of the use, or misuse, of the suggestions made herein. None of the views or suggestions in this book are intended to replace medical opinion from a doctor. If you have concerns about your health or that of a child in your care, please seek advice from a medical professional.

Worry
Monsters

This book belongs to

Find your battle cry!

Worry can be tough to beat, but you don't have to do it all by yourself! All the people you love and trust are in your team to help you.

Why not come up with a
battle cry to help you feel brave
so you can beat worry!

I CAN
DO THIS!

I NEVER
GIVE UP!

Pick one of
these for
your battle
cry, or write
your own in
the spaces.

I'M
GREAT!

5

The Worry Animal

If your worry was an animal, what would it look like?

- [ ] Number of heads
- [ ] Number of legs
- [ ] Number of arms
- [ ] Is it hairy?
- [ ] Is it furry?
- [ ] Does it have feathers?
- [ ] Does it have scales like a snake or a fish?
- [ ] Does it have smooth skin like a mole?
- [ ] Does it have horns like a Triceratops?
- [ ] Is it smiling?

And what is this fantastical fabulous beast called?

_____

Draw your worry animal here:

Love your differences

We are all different – that's what makes us all so special and unique!

Here's a fun game to play with your grown-up. Write your names at the top of each column, then go through the different favourite things and draw or write them in the spaces.

Add your names in here

FAVOURITE THING		
Favourite food		
Favourite animal		

Favourite colour		
Favourite toy		
Favourite TV show		
Favourite clothes		
Favourite cuddly toy		
Favourite film		
Favourite book		
Favourite game		

How many matches do you have? write the number here _____

Even though you have different favourite things, you still love to spend time together. It's OK to like different things — it's the only way you can be truly you!

You're a star!

Sometimes worries arrive suddenly and you can't think of anything else. Breathing like a star helps you shine again by launching those worries into galaxies far, far away.

Trace over the star lines, breathing in while you trace to the tip, then pause, breathing out while you trace to the centre.

Do this as many times as you need to, in as many colours as you can manage.

Soon your fabulously colourful star will twinkle your worries away!

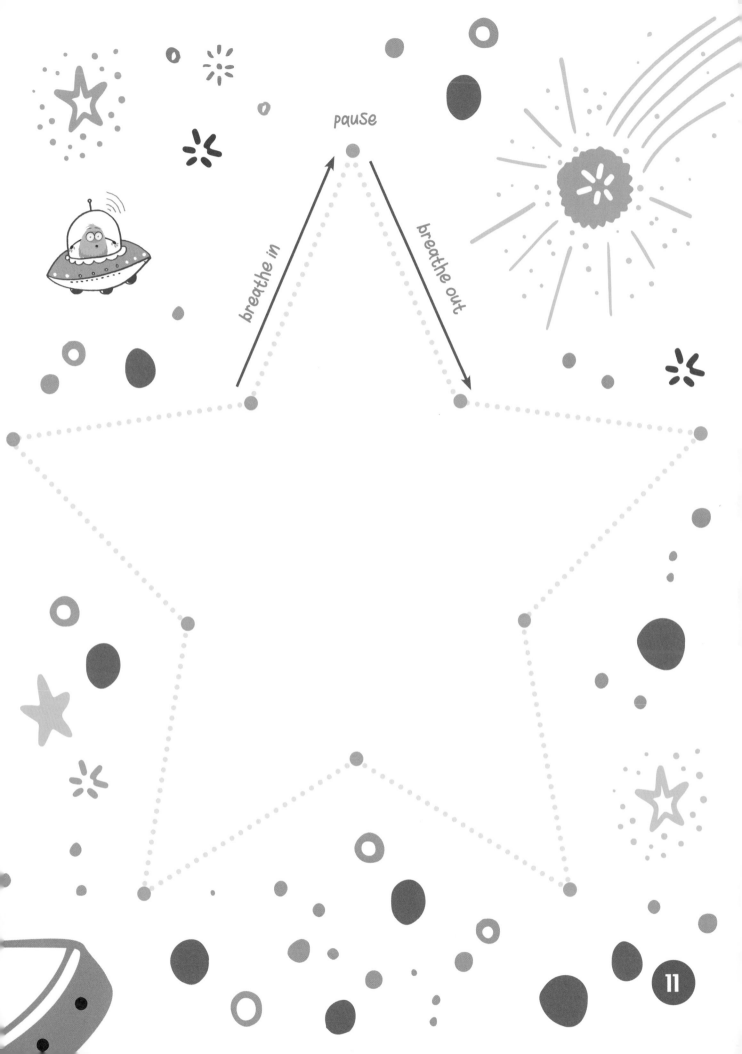

pause

breathe in

breathe out

11

Flurry of Worries

Draw a line from cloud to cloud, answering the questions as you fly through the beautiful sky, then colour them in.

IS it Something you can change?

HOW MANY WORRIES DO YOU HAVE?

1

More than 1

choose your biggest worry.

12

Box of socks

This smart little monster worries about wearing odd socks. Can you help him find his way into this box to find the matching sock?

If you have any worries you can write them down in this box. Have a look at what you have written in a week's time and if any of the worries don't worry you anymore, cross them out! Then try again the week after that.

Or you could find an empty box, or jar, decorate it and use it to post your worries in!

Worried words

Some monsters are feeling anxious.
Help them feel better by finding the
words in the wordsearch.

Q	U	D	H	U	U	J	F	O	D	H	A	N	L	K
G	T	R	Y	R	N	O	I	A	C	R	N	N	H	I
U	L	I	B	R	S	I	C	K	C	U	G	O	G	F
S	D	O	R	T	G	V	G	U	Z	H	R	E	E	W
B	T	B	P	Y	X	E	D	H	E	D	Y	R	Q	H
H	S	M	N	J	A	R	G	F	T	M	T	C	V	J
T	A	Y	Z	X	S	U	Y	I	H	M	G	E	U	D
U	Z	M	Q	V	B	S	D	D	L	W	A	A	P	N
M	S	V	A	A	T	I	A	G	T	N	L	R	S	D
M	H	E	A	D	A	C	H	E	Q	E	O	G	E	U
Y	K	O	F	X	P	V	Q	T	V	Z	N	S	T	S
A	W	X	J	Q	N	T	K	Y	Q	I	J	S	Q	E
C	Q	W	B	J	P	P	S	E	C	T	I	R	E	D
H	Y	D	B	V	D	X	G	M	H	R	V	B	N	A
E	H	N	A	H	N	A	E	Y	T	K	S	F	W	N

Tummy ache	Upset
Nightmares	Angry
Headache	Tired
Fidgety	Achy
Tense	Sick

Remember to talk to a grown-up if you ever feel any of these things.

Worry worm

I am a very little worm
But I am here for you.
You can tell me all your worries
And I will listen too.
Worms are best at listening,
worries are best out loud.
So tell me all your worries
And we'll banish your dark cloud.

I'm here with you,
you're safe.

Follow the wiggly lines to find out what each worm is saying to you.

What's something we could do to help you feel better?

Let's draw your worry.

Do you want to try and get rid of the worried energy by jumping or running?

Where is the worry?

What does it feel like in your body?
Can you show where it is? How big does it feel?

?

?

or here?

Perhaps
it is here?

?

?

?

Is it here?

worry worry worry worry worry worry worry worry worry WORRY worry worry worry WORRY worry worry worry worry worry WORRY worry worry WORRY worry worry worry

How many worries are bothering these monsters?

21

Have a chat

What would you like to say to your worry?
What might your worry say back to you?

carry on the conversation!

22

Dear worry...

23

Candle Colouring

Help this monster to colour all his emotion candles. What colour will worry be?

happiness   **sadness**   **anger**

fear

calm

worry

Rain, Rain, Go Away...

Join the dots to see who's trying to shelter from the rain.

Remember the feeling so you will know what it is when it happens again.

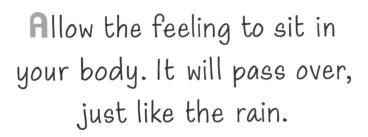

Allow the feeling to sit in your body. It will pass over, just like the rain.

Inspect the feeling — how does it feel in your body?

No, you are not the worry — this feeling will go away.

Monster Mantras

A mantra is a few words you can say
to yourself when a worry visits you.

Choose your favourite mantra and decide
which worried monster needs to say it
— draw a line between them.
Write down any you can think of
in the box opposite.

I am brave.

My best is
good enough.

I am safe.

I am safe.

My best is good enough.

I am brave.

I am calm.

I am loved.

_____

_____

Find some coloured beads and a pipe
cleaner. Thread on one bead at a time,
saying your favourite mantra until you
have a bracelet. Wear it as a daily
reminder to think positive thoughts.

Fluttery Butterflies

Some little monsters know they have a worry because it flutters in their tummies, feeling like butterflies.

Colour in these butterflies and think of any worries you may have. Draw your butterflies in the big butterfly net so they are caught and taken away — big ones to represent large worries and smaller ones for less worrying worries. Remember to listen to your breathing as you do this.

Page 14

Page 18–19

Page 16

Page 21

Answer: 24

Page 26

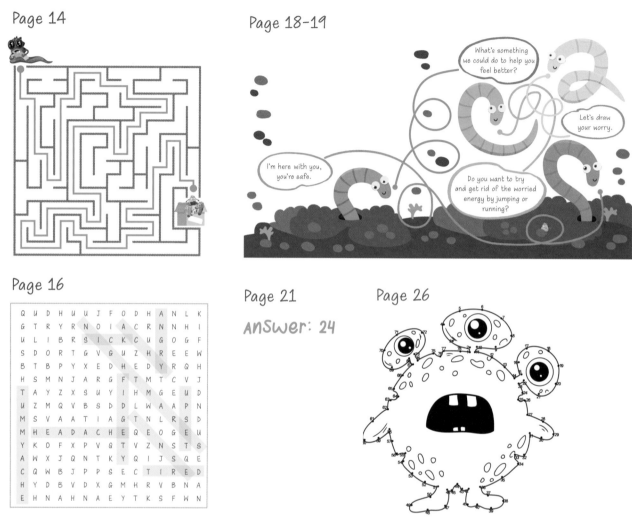

Did you spot me hiding on every page?

Have you enjoyed this book?

If so, why not write a review on your favourite website?
If you're interested in finding out more about our books,
find us on Facebook at **Summersdale Publishers**,
on Twitter at **@Summersdale** and on Instagram
at **@summersdalebooks** and get in touch.
We'd love to hear from you!

Thanks very much for buying this Summersdale book.

www.summersdale.com